# T.S. CHERRY

# Answers II

*Coronovisrus and Passover*

Copyright © 2020 by T.S. Cherry

All rights reserved. No part of this publication may be reproduced, stored or transmitted in any form or by any means, electronic, mechanical, photocopying, recording, scanning, or otherwise without written permission from the publisher. It is illegal to copy this book, post it to a website, or distribute it by any other means without permission.

T.S. Cherry asserts the moral right to be identified as the author of this work.

First edition

This book was professionally typeset on Reedsy.
Find out more at reedsy.com

# Contents

I   A Significant Passover

1   A Significant Passover   3

II   Keeping the Yeast Out of the Home & Body!

2   Keeping the Yeast Out of the House!   17

# I

# A Significant Passover

*There's never been a better time to access God than in critical moments like this. This is the season when God is most active, will show you Who He is, and has answers for you. This is when you get to understand the difference between man's solutions and God's solutions.*

# 1

# A Significant Passover

It is good to take a quick look at the times we're in right now. I'm sure that some of the things I have already written about are beginning to unfold.

Beloved, this is the moment to be able to access God in a way that you've never been able to access Him. This is the moment to be able to get information from God that you may not even have thought to access before.

Now, you'll ask the hard questions that perhaps you wouldn't have asked before. This is the season when God is most active; the season when God has answers for you. This is when God shows you Who He is. This is when you get to understand the difference between man's solutions and God's solutions.

**A Significant Passover**

Now, we're living in the time of the Passover, and people are trying to understand the Passover like never before.

We've been told the children's version of these stories for so long, but the practical aspect of what's going on is not often taught in our churches and synagogues. So, the reasons behind what we do for

Passover sometimes has left us. Consequently, we find that we're deep into the observances without adequate knowledge of why.

It's like the story of the woman who cuts off the ends of the ham before cooking it. Then her two daughters, who saw her do it, also cook the ham the same way she does by cutting off the ends. When asked why they did it that way, the daughters had no explanation but only to say it was the way their mother did it. It had become a tradition for the family.

When they decided to go back and ask their mum why she prepared the ham that way, she explained that she did it because the ham didn't fit in her little pan at that time. Her daughters had a bigger pan and could change that tradition, but they didn't because they didn't even know in the first place, why it was done.

In other words, they had a pan that was big enough for their hams to go in and didn't need to cut off the sap. But you see, if you don't know the original reason why some things were done, you just keep on repeating them needlessly.

We see a lot of this in the Passover season.

**Living Sacrifice**

Let us take a look at the primary purpose of the Passover.

I'll veer off a little and talk about the familiar story of Cain and Abel.

Both Cain and Abel brought an offering of their choice to the Lord. Cain offered something he grew from the ground. He wanted to create his way to God, which was the same problem that existed later on at the Tower of Babel when the people wanted to find their way to God.

On the other hand, we know that Abel stayed steadfast to what he was taught. He observed the requirements of God, which was to live off the Word, and not just the Word, but every Word that proceeded out of the Mouth of God. He offered a living sacrifice. And if we're honest, that is essentially the Passover story.

Now, like Abel, when we're creating our Passover meal, what we are essentially doing is, we are offering our sacrifice. We are saying that we're not going to be like Egypt, we're not going to offer that which grew from the ground because we have learned better, and are teaching our children better, too.

At least, we now understand that even though we are eating the lamb as a living sacrifice, we are supposed to be the living sacrifice.

**A Better Understanding**

We should have an overall understanding that God is essentially Lord over our lives and that we are meant to submit to His decisions over ours, even when we don't understand. So the lamb in the Passover is simply a picture of our being able to lay down our lives as a sacrifice from generation to generation.

When you look at it from the point of utmost surrender, you see that God wants more than just your Sunday morning. He wants every second, every minute, and every day of your life. He wants the way you interact with other people. He wants the way you do business. He wants the way you give medical treatments. He wants the way you build your communities. He wants all of that so that He can guide or direct you.

God wants you to walk with the Holy Spirit so that you can have a compass. He wants to shade some light into your life, so you don't try to navigate your way in the dark. And that's where we see the difference between Cain and Abel.

Abel had seen the light. He knew there was a better way. It may not have been in his culture, but he was exposed to the light and had come to a better understanding.

Cain hadn't seen the light. He was still offering up the same things he had always offered. He wasn't spiritually enlightened. Beyond that, he hated his brother for seeing the light and having a better understanding than he did.

Today, we see 'Cain and Abel' play out before us daily: religion versus light; man's ideas versus God's enlightenment; problems versus real solutions.

**Baal: A Different Teaching**

If you look at it critically, both Cain and Abel were taught essentially by the same person – their mother. And the truth is, mothers have to be the primary teachers of their children, and not television, environment, or culture. Mothers must teach their children to navigate this world like Cain and Abel's mother taught them.

But you see, despite their mother's teaching, Cain chose to go his way. He chose a path different from what he was taught. He offered up to God whatever he wanted, but Abel followed the right path.

In Cain's jealousy, he went ahead and murdered Abel. Nevertheless, when you look at the descendants of Abel and that of Cain, you see a major difference. One is the progenitor of a religion that has God at the center of it while the other is a progenitor of a religion of the East.

This is important!

Both religions originated from the same place. The difference is how they interpret the information they have. It is not that one has a better Bible than the other. It's simple! They have the same Bible; the difference is how they interpret it.

Baal was a god worshipped in many ancient Middle Eastern communities, especially among the Canaanites. *Baal* is not a Hebrew word. Its origin is semantic. The word in its original translation means "husband." And you know, the curse on the woman was that she would submit under her "husband."

This would mean that her punishment was to submit to the religion or culture, which was Baal. And Baal is, of course, an interpretation or manipulation of, not just God's Word but His understanding and solutions. It's just a different way of teaching.

That was Eve's punishment.

So, we see that when she gives birth, half of her lineage submits to God and the other half submits to Baal, which represents the ways of the world. It's like raising two children, and one child is saved while the other child is not. Essentially, that's what Eve experienced.

**Getting the Leaven Out**

We understand that the Passover is about the lamb, and it's about making sure that we are offering a living sacrifice. But there's also one primary thing that is important and is done all the way up into the day of Passover. That is getting the leaven out of the house.

There are always spiritual as well as practical applications. The spiritual application is that yeast represents sin. We want to get sin out of our homes.

The practical application, on the other hand, is that yeast in the body breeds disease. In other words, the more you like to eat bread, cheese, wine ect. the more grounds the disease has to grow and feed within you.

It has been proven that a sick body is more acidic. And in acidic environments, yeast essentially grows faster. In times like these, it is both recommended and advisable that we abstain from yeast, and I have written extensively on this in another article I'll love you to read in the following chapters.

For this time and period, I am restraining from bread; call it a fast if you will. But my Passover agenda is to refrain from bread and to try and get my body to be as alkaline as possible.

This is what I believe some people did in the Spanish Flu: They took one tablespoon of baking soda every day to make the body more alkaline. I take a bath with bath bombs made without citric acid which are made mainly of baking soda daily.

**Keep Fear Out!**
Another thing you must constantly do is to keep fear out. You don't want the enemy to use this as an advantage. You need to be one step ahead of him and put your fears aside. This is a time where you need to lay on your face, seek God, and be responsible.

David said, "Though I walk through the valley of the shadow of death, I shall fear no evil." In the world, fears become 'yeast.' Thus, you must remove all fear from your body, by resisting what science calls fight or flight, that causes fear.

Keep fear out!

**A Real Battle**
Sometimes we fail to measure darkness by its impact on us and those around us. But sooner or later, darkness always lets us know it is there. It tries to secure a home in our fear, in our tiredness, in our inability to measure its presence. The World of Darkness is just as real as the world of light and they are both fighting for the place of being Lord over us.

Invisible enemies have one thing in common: They study you while you fail to study them. So, with every attack, the enemy evolves and gets better at what he does. Make no mistakes beloved; light and darkness are very real.

The Bible tells us many secrets about the lord of darkness and his desire to rule. There are certain environments where darkness thrives. You know, sometimes we call cancer darkness, but it is not limited to cancer. It takes pride in getting you to eat certain kinds of food. These cravings affect your pH balance, and when that happens, the body becomes more susceptible to diseases.

Just as I've already pointed out, the Torah teaches us that during the Passover, we are to get all the yeast out of our home. In like manner, we are to get all yeast out of our body. If you go through these teachings without realizing that yeast brings disease, you can be negatively impacted.

Like cancer, yeast grows and you feed it the same way you feed bread - with flour and sugar. So, the Torah is telling us to get all the yeast out of our bodies, and the things that feed it - sugar and flour.

**Light and Darkness**

Our lack of knowledge has destroyed a lot of people. But this is something that we have the power to overcome; something that we have the power to change.

In Judaism, darkness and light are considered two different realms or two different worlds. But the Bible makes it abundantly clear that God reveals the secrets of darkness. So, if you understand that darkness has secrets, it means that God can reveal to you the darkness behind the disease.

God can reveal to you the things you need to do to help you get through this disease. He can reveal to you the plans of the enemy, even an invisible one. He can help you plan practical things that you can do, like growing seeds, using baking soda as a way to make your body more alkaline, etc.

The truth, beloved, is that in your darkest hour, you need light.

**Come Out on the Other Side**

I will never forget when I was grieving for my son and I went to a pastor. He was recommended because he had lost a child. But I realized he hadn't seen the light. He couldn't help me. He had experienced it, but he hadn't come out on the other side.

Now, there is something important about going through it and seeing the light. That helps you understand that sometimes life happens and sometimes we lose people. In such cases, how do we get through our grief?

Grief is such a dark place. It goes through the fiber of who we are and makes us question everything we thought we knew; every experience we thought we had.

Grief will tear one side of you from the other. It is one of the few things that does not care who you are. Grief affects the highest as well as the lowest person.

Well, whether it is the loss of a child you loved or the loss of your identity, God wants you to see a new light, and come out on the other side. But how do you know you have seen the light? By proffering or providing solutions.

If you look at the majority of inventions and the solutions that have come to the world, even in horrific times, many of them admit that God gave it to them. And if you pay a bit of attention, you will discover that the Jews, who have practically gone through a lot, have quite a greater number of scientific inventions.

The Jewish people have made such enormous contributions to Science, Medicine, Economics, etc., that the secular world cannot claim ignorance. The truth is, that's the way God sends solutions. He sends it through people being able to create solutions that have never been created before.

So then, it's not just about being able to pray your way through your circumstance; it's about seeing the light and being able to create solutions. It's about being able to go get your brother. It's about being able to feed people; it's about being able to help people; it's about being able to save lives.

**Balance it with Prayer**

As much as there are things you can do to help give you a powerful body, you must also find a balance between them and prayer. Think about the battle between Israel and the Amalekites. For as long as Moses the man of God kept his hands up, Israel would win. But when his hands came down, Amalek would begin to gain power over Israel.

So, it was more like, if the man of God stopped praying, they would lose the battle. That was because it was not simply a one-sided battle. It was a blend of doing what needed to be done spiritually while fighting physically.

That's the way it is with us today. No matter how much we can do to stay healthy and resist infections, there must be a balance of prayer to keep us on the victory side. 50% of doing what needs to be done in prayer, and 50% of doing what needs to be done nutritionally and medically, get us there.

You must understand how to address things in the natural - the medications you should take, putting on the mask, getting the yeast out of your house, etc. These are natural things that you can do. Then, align yourself with the power of prayer. You can't do one without the other, both are needed to be able to handle the secret of darkness.

**Thinking Differently**

Think for a moment on the scenario in John's Gospel about the man who was born blind. The disciples of Jesus wanted to know if it was the fault of his mother or father. Jesus said it was none of those, but that God would be glorified.

Today we are in a situation where blindness has covered the earth, and we're busy trying to find out, "Who is responsible for this?" It is not necessarily the mothers or the fathers who raised us. Rather, God allowed this! That's all Christ is saying. God has allowed it for such a time as this so that when He takes the blinders off, you will be able to see the difference between God and the systems of the world.

In times like these, rather than concern ourselves with who's at fault or who's not, we need to begin to think differently. We may not be able to congregate as a church but we can still be connected.

As pastors, for instance, we must be able to give our people some practical things to help ease their fears. Get into holistic health. Talk about controlled breathing if they're having trouble breathing. Talk about making sure that they have their face mask on at all times. Let people have important information because it saves lives.

A lot of communities are running short of food, and some farmers say they have stuff in the fields going bad. This is the time to get together with the farmers and say, hey, can we put on our mask and come pick the food that you have out in the fields going bad? We can pick the food and distribute it to the people at our church through the drive-through lines.

You can speak to some restaurant owners who have a drive-through, and find out if you can utilize their drive-through to be able to hand out goods to certain people. You can partner with some people and get these things done. It's just a matter of seeing what's available, looking at the problem smartly, and finding solutions.

That is what Christ is about. Christ is about bringing light into the problem. Light is the solution. It is the ability to help, and find a way. It is not about putting people at risk; that is selfish. It is about finding out if people are safe. It is about taking time out to check if they have their medications.

I love what one particular community did. They blocked off the village and got some persons who go out to get everything they need, then bring it to everybody. That's a good solution. You should also identify and do some problem solving using practical approaches that can help in your neighborhood.

Begin to look two, three, four months down the road. Prepare your people. Get seeds together. There are some companies right now that are only selling to farmers. Get those seeds and plant them. Also, give some seeds to other people to plant. And it can be just as simple as giving them a seed that's planted in a self-watering pot and dropping it off on their front porch. That could be tomatoes, cucumbers, etc.

A self-watering pot is just a matter of two buckets with a plastic cup in the middle and a piece of PVC pipe. If you go to the store it might cost you $30, but if you make it yourself, it'll cost you $2. So, for $2 and some cents, you can grow the tomato seeds by putting them in cups, so that when the time comes, you could be able to hand out tomato and cucumber plants, so that people can have fresh vegetables.

Think about it, your health depends on being able to have access to fresh foods. I know you have some canned foods, but you do need fresh produce.

**Recognize the Light**

If the world has a problem, you have to look around because darkness does not take God by surprise. Somewhere, God has already created a solution, which is the understanding of darkness and discovering the light.

Isaiah 45:2-3 says, *"I will go before you,...and level the mountains. I will smash down gates of bronze and cut through bars of iron. And I will give you treasures hidden in the darkness—secret riches. I will do this so you may know that I am the Lord, the God of Israel, the one who calls you by name."* At this time, a lot of people are displaced. So, you must think of different things that you can do, probably a little different from the norm.

I heard a story about people who were in the 9/11 towers. There was a lady who was in charge, and she said to others, "We are going up to the roof." She was the team leader and the people were following her. But one young man said, "No, I've seen this before. We go down, and go out." He said, "I'm not going up; I'm going down."

Going up was protocol. The protocol called for them to go to the roof and wait for an airplane to come and rescue them. But he knew when to break off from what protocol called for. He was able to survive, and those who followed him were able to survive. That was because he took a different route. He followed a different path from what had been previously outlined.

It was protocol. It was what was put in place. It was the best information they had about how to survive if there ever was an attack. But that information was wrong. And many times amid the moment, you need somebody that knows when the given information is wrong. You need to know when to follow protocol and go up to the roof to wait for an airplane or when to break protocol and walk away. Everyone that followed the young man, lived. But everyone that followed the leader, died.

That is a very, very hard lesson to learn. They only had moments to make that decision. And sometimes that's all we ever get when the time comes. You only get one chance to decide either to follow protocol or break from protocol. That's all you get. It's a powerful lesson. It's a lesson that some people have to learn the hard way.

I see a world of darkness, but in the darkness, God is saying, "Let there be light." However, the thing is, you need to recognize the light amid the darkness because it won't always come from where you think it should come. It may not come through who you think it should come, or the method you think it should come.

The light may not always come through religion. Sometimes it will come through science. But it may not always come through science. Sometimes it will come through religion. Yes, that is the truth. Sometimes it will come through schools, too. But whichever way it comes, you must have the flexibility to be able to recognize the light that's in the darkness. That is what is going to save you, in times like these.

# II

# Keeping the Yeast Out of the Home & Body!

*Preparing for **Passover** usually begins a full month before **Passover** arrives, just after the festival of Purim. ... days of **Passover**, we make a special effort to remove **leaven** entirely from our **homes and bodies**, ... This includes washing **out** the freezer as well. ... Let us then "**keep** the feast,"*

2

## Keeping the Yeast Out of the House!

While we try to grapple with the situation at hand, I'd love to share a bit on something I think is very important for each person to consider, and that is Keeping the Yeast Out of the House.

On the last day of Passover, I thought deeply about a few things; and this year's Passover was like none other. The current plague has shade light on our tradition and caused us to experience Christ in a new way. A lot of things have changed for me, and I was able to bring them to the modern day context, but I'd love to focus particularly on *yeast and hyssop*.

Speaking about the Passover, Exodus 12:14-15 (NIV) says, *"This is a day you are to commemorate; for the generations to come you shall celebrate it as a festival to the Lord — a lasting ordinance.* **For seven days you are to eat bread made without yeast. On the first day remove the yeast from your houses,...***"

Now, I'll like you to pay attention to the sentences in bold for a while. First, it says, *"...you are to eat bread made without yeast."* This is very significant for a time like this. And it doesn't just have to be limited to bread but also aged cheese, mushrooms, yeast-processed and cured meats, dried fruits, gravy, and stock cubes, processed fruit juices, vinegar containing ingredients, alcohol (brewer's yeast), etc.

Why is God's command on what I'll call "yeast abstinence" important for us at this time? Well, it will interest you to know that yeast is a potential harbor of viruses. A paper by Richard Yuqi Zhao of the Institute of Human Virology, University of Maryland School of Medicine, Baltimore, explains that some yeasts are natural hosts for viruses. Many positive sense (+) RNA viruses and some DNA viruses replicate with various levels in yeasts.

You can see with me that the Bible is right!

I am aware that America tends to consume large amounts of yeast, but you can refrain from eating bread and other high yeast products at this time. The truth is, you lose nothing by doing a "yeast fast," that is, keep yeast out of your body for some time. That sacrifice is simple for most of us to do.

The second thing that Exodus 12:14-15 says is that you are to *"...remove the yeast from your houses,..."* So, God is saying to clean your house and make sure that there is no yeast or diseases found there. The emphasis here is eliminating the disease-causing agents from your house, and there are many ways to do this.

I have heard, for instance, that the virus can be trapped on the bottom of your feet. So, if you leave your shoes off at the door, there is the possibility that it does not get into your house. And if you have a wooden floor and other such surfaces, they are very easy to sterilize, wipe down and clean off.

You will also find that the best environment for yeasts to grow is also the best environment for disease to grow - that is in dark, dirty and damp places. So, you may need to open the windows and also wipe things clean, so that the disease does not have a comfortable place to thrive.

You see! The biblical "keep the yeast out of your house" can have a very practical application in this season.

**Pray and Keep Positive**

Keeping the yeast out of your home is not just about cleaning the house but also cleaning your mind. You must equally keep the yeast out of your mind, by praying and keeping positive so that your negative thoughts do not have grounds to breed.

In times like this, you must focus on the positive. Maybe you have to post positive stickers or notes from faith-building Scriptures or listen to God's Word over and over. But do whatever you need to do to keep your mind focused on the positive.

Yes, I know you want to be aware of what's going on, pay attention to the news, and keep up with what is happening. You may be mindful of the news, but you should not allow it to control your emotions.

A lot of times, to keep positive, I pray and play praise and worship music in my house. I mostly turn it on loud, so that the music can be heard all through the house. That way, there is a positive atmosphere in the house that keeps all the negativities away.

**Avoid Grief**

Listen, this is for many of us tough times, but you must do your best to avoid grief. I need you to understand that grief weakens the immune system, and can put you in danger.

If you know a little about my story or read it in any of my books, then you probably have heard about my son's death and the lessons that I learned at that moment. If I had succumbed to grief, I wouldn't be here today.

In this time where I have lost loved ones, I have to be very mindful. Probably the time will come to grieve, but that time is not now. Sometimes, certain things like a video that my family sends around tend to trigger something, but I catch and guard myself because I understand that now is not the time to grieve. Instead, I keep my mind focused like a soldier in the war front. I put my grief away until my life is no longer in danger.

**Hyssop Helps**

The final thing I want to discuss here is the idea of hyssop in the Bible. I'm sure you are familiar with the word 'hyssop' at least if not anywhere else, in Psalms 51:7 where David prayed, *"Purge me with hyssop, and I shall be clean;"*

Hyssop is an interesting choice as a cleansing agent. It is an herb that grows just under three feet in height, producing clusters of variously colored flowers. The short, cut stems of the plant can be gathered into bunches, and in the Old Testament, these bunches were used for several purposes.

Exodus 12:21-22 (NLT) says, *"Then Moses called all the elders of Israel together and said to them, "Go, pick out a lamb or young goat for each of your families, and slaughter the Passover animal. Drain the blood into a basin. Then take a bundle of hyssop branches and dip it into the blood. Brush the hyssop across the top and sides of the doorframes of your houses. And no one may go out through the door until morning."*

In the above Passover event of Exodus 12, God directed that the Israelites dip a bunch of hyssop into the blood of the Passover Lamb, and sprinkle or brush on the doorposts and lintel of each home. Also, in Leviticus and Numbers, hyssop was used as part of sacrificial ceremonies. The hyssop was always tied into bunches for use in sprinkling the blood of the sacrificed animal.

Research shows that hyssop contains valuable antiseptic or cleansing properties that would "disinfect" a contaminated person or his possessions. Thus, it is beneficial to take a bath or cleanse in hyssop. It is said that the Romans used it because they believed it helped protect them against plagues. The herb is useful today for many health issues including, digestive and intestinal as well as respiratory problems.

It is useful for liver and gallbladder conditions, intestinal pain, and loss of appetite. It can also be used to eliminate coughs, prevent the common cold and respiratory infections, soothe sore throats, and remedy asthma.

Today we don't use hyssop for sprinkling, so you may not have it around, but you do have access to bleach. So, as you receive some supplies at your door, take some bleach, put it in a spray bottle, leave it on the front porch of your house for at least three hours and then go outside.

The virus lives in the air for about three hours, and so when someone drops something for you at the front porch, you can leave it there for about three hours, spray it out with some bleach, and then bring it into the house. That provides added protection for you and your family.

In conclusion, we can do our part of cleaning the yeast out of the house, as well as make sure that it does not grow in our thoughts and minds through grief and negative thinking. We can also put the ordinance of sprinkling with hyssop into modern day use and provide added protection for ourselves and our loved ones in the midst of the chaos and uncertainty.

www.ingramcontent.com/pod-product-compliance
Lightning Source LLC
Chambersburg PA
CBHW050205130526
44591CB00034B/2161